Purry Logic

For Mark, Clare, and Jamie

Jane Seabrook

Furry Logic

TEN SPEED PRESS
Berkeley | Toronto

Delusions of grandeur make me feel

a lot better about myself.

I can do without the essentials,

but I must have my luxuries.

I prefer   *the kind of work*

I can do with my feet up

and my eyes closed.

Do the *absolute* minimum.

Always. Try to do even less.

As a matter of fact,

I haven't moved since you

left this morning.

It might look like I'm doing nothing,

but at the cellular level I'm really

quite busy.

The trouble with doing nothing

is that you don't know

when you're finished.

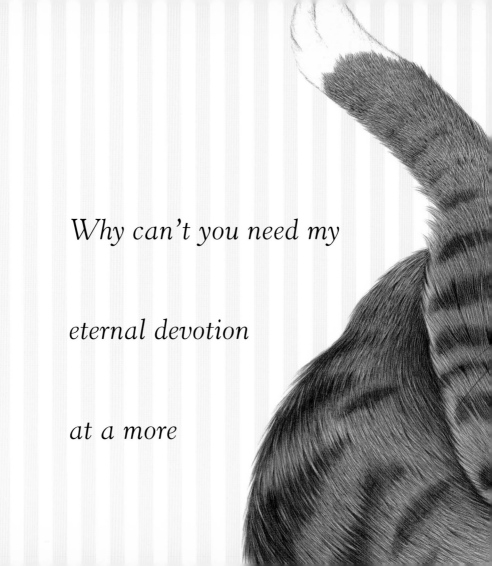

Why can't you need my

eternal devotion

at a more

convenient time?

My only purpose in this life

is to rest and recover

from my previous lives.

If I like it, it's mine.

If I saw it first, it's mine.

If it's in my paws, it's mine.

If it was already dead, it's yours.

Bird:

canned food with wings but no can.

What canary?

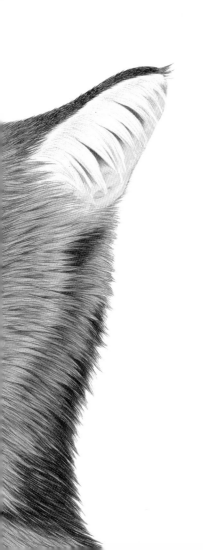

Note to self:

When scratching

the furniture,

it is easier to get

forgiveness

than permission.

If you didn't make the rules,

just

ignore

them.

Now that's what I call catnip!

Purr

your way out of trouble.

When asked to come

out from under the furniture,

silently count to three...

hundred thousand.

I hear the call to do nothing,

and am doing my best

to answer it.

Consciousness:

that annoying time between naps.

Hey,

keep it down. We only had 20

 hours of sleep yesterday.

Who's in control of this bed?

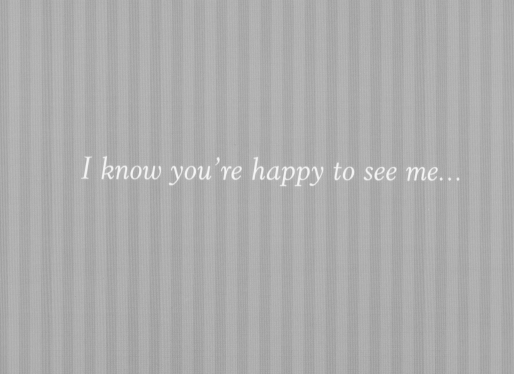

I know you're happy to see me…

just open the can.

What part of MEOW

don't you understand?

Neighbors: the best way to

get a five-course meal.

When

fat,

arrange

yourself

in slim

poses.

Never feed me anything

that doesn't match the carpet.

You're the warmest piece of

furniture I know.

The best things in life are

furry.

Have you really

done enough

for your cat today?

Ready for my dinner now –

you may carry me to my bowl.

Artist's Notes

We are all cat-mad in my family. We must be, since we have four felines who rule our lives. In order of bossiness they are: Bean, Maisie, Fizz, and Philby.

Philby, an elderly British Blue, cannot stand the other three, and no amount of coaxing can convince her otherwise. (There was no way she would appear in the group photo.) As far as she is concerned, she was here first and those three Birmans are just imposters. So Philby has abandoned the house to the Birmans and has taken up residence in the barn—a very mouse-free barn—and now everyone is happy.

They are all utterly adorable of course, a great inspiration for this book, and perfect models when I needed to check the intricacies of the very short fur on the bridge of a cat's nose, for example. If you want to paint cats, it pays to know these things!

I hope you have enjoyed this collection of thirty or so eclectic cats and I always enjoy receiving your comments and suggestions via the website, www.purrylogic.com.

Best wishes,

Jane.

For more information, including
how to purchase any of the original
paintings that appear in this book,
visit www.purrylogic.com.

Purry Logic Who's Who

There are some cat breeds so extreme that I didn't dare paint them because people might think I made them up! However, I did try to paint as many different breeds as possible and I've named them here—with apologies to breeders if I get any wrong!

1. Picasso, domestic tabby 2. Marmite, Havana Brown

3. Skooter, red domestic tabby 4. Winston, Ojos Azules

5. Boston, domestic tabby 6. Benson, domestic bi-color

7. Gizmo, domestic longhair 8. Cisco, domestic tabby

9. Otis, Calico British Shorthair 10. Minette, red domestic tabby kitten 11. Bird, snack, plaything 12. Pickle, Seal Point Snowshoe 13. Ms. Demeanor, domestic tabby 14. Harpo, Bi-color British Shorthair 15. Casey, domestic tabby 16. Baxter, domestic bi-color 17. Reba, Brown Tabby Bengal 18. Meomyo, domestic tabby 19. Ozzie, domestic tabby 20. Tula, Seal Point Siamese

Purry Logic Who's Who

21. Tao, Red Point Siamese 22. Lulu, Shaded Silver Persian
23. Elmo, domestic bi-color 24. Seymour, Shaded Golden
Persian 25. Sherlock, Bi-Color Persian 26. Scarlett, red
domestic tabby 27. Nana Yaw, Seal Color Point Persian
28. Pepper, domestic tabby 29. Maisie, Seal Point Birman
30. Dexter, American Shorthair 31. Zappa, Burmilla

Jane Seabrook is an illustrator and designer who lives in
Auckland, New Zealand. She shares her life with her husband,
two teenage children, and a growing menagerie of assorted
animals.

Other Books by Jane Seabrook

Furry Logic: A Guide to Life's Little Challenges

Furry Logic Parenthood

Furry Logic Laugh at Life

The Pick of Furry Logic

Furry Logic Wild Wisdom

For more information visit www.furrylogicbooks.com.

28.   29.   30.   31.

Acknowledgments

Grateful thanks to Ashleigh Brilliant for permission to reproduce the following quotations that appear in this book: "I can do without the essentials, but I must have my luxuries." "I prefer the kind of work I can do with my feet up and my eyes closed." "Why can't you need my eternal devotion at some (a) more convenient time?" "I hear the call to do nothing, and am doing my best to answer it." "Who's in command (control) of this bed?" "The best things in life are furry." "Have you really done enough for your cat today?" "My only purpose in this life is to rest and recover from my previous lives" is derived from the original Pot-Shot # 4090, "Relax! Your only purpose in this life may be to rest and recover from some previous life."

The above quotations are from the Ashleigh Brilliant Pot-Shot series. For more information, visit www.ashleighbrilliant.com.

Grateful thanks to New Holland Publishers, Sydney, Australia, for permission to reproduce the following quotations from *Cattitude*, by Geoff Bartlett and Gudrun Reiss: "As a matter of fact, I haven't moved since you left this morning." "Hey, keep it down. I (we) only had 20 hours (of) sleep yesterday." "You're the warmest piece of furniture I know." "Ready for my dinner now—you may carry me to my bowl" is derived from "I'm ready for dinner now—you may carry me to the dining room."

Other quotations appeared or are quoted in the following publications:

"Delusions of grandeur make me feel a lot better about myself." (Jane Wagner) in *The 637 Best Things Anybody Ever Said*, Robert Byrne, Ballantine Books, UK. "Bird—canned food with wings but no can." (Anon.) in *Utterly Adorable Cats*, a Helen Exley Giftbook, Exley Publications Ltd., UK.

Thank you also to readers who sent in cat quotes, especially to Kelli McConkey for "What part of MEOW don't you understand?"

While every effort has been made to trace copyright holders of the quotations, the publisher would be very pleased to hear from any not acknowledged here to make amends in future printings.

Thank you to everyone at Ten Speed Press for their support and encouragement, especially Lorena Jones, Lisa Westmoreland, and Kristine Standley.

Thank you also to Alex Trimbach and Troy Caltaux at Image Centre in Auckland, New Zealand, and to Joy Willis and Ricky Cheng at Phoenix Offset.

Ten Speed Press
P O Box 7123, Berkeley, California 94707, United States
www.tenspeed.com

Distributed in Canada by Ten Speed Press Canada, in South Africa by Real Books,
and in the United Kingdom and Europe by Publishers Group UK.

Library of Congress Cataloging-in-Publication Data
Seabrook, Jane.
Purry logic / by Jane Seabrook.
p. cm.
Summary: "An all-feline collection of adorable illustrations, humorous sayings, and cattitude
from the creator of Furry Logic"—Provided by publisher.
ISBN 978-1-58008-904-3
1. Cats—Humor. 2. Cats—Pictorial works. I. Title.
PN6231.C23S43 2008
818'.602—dc22   2008004723

Printed in China
First printing, 2008

1 2 3 4 5 6 7 8 9 10 — 12 11 10 09 08